The Best of the Devil's Dictionary

The Best of the Devil's Dictionary

By

Ambrose Bierce

Edited by Bart Schneider

Kelly's Cove Press

Berkeley

Published by Kelly's Cove Press
2733 Prince Street
Berkeley, CA 94705
www.kellyscovepress.com

Published in the United States of America
ISBN 978-1-61364-455-3

Library of Congress Control Number: 2011936926

First printing

Cover and interior design by Lynn Phelps

Cover painting: *Standing Figure*, 1970, by Nathan Oliveria
Used by permission of the Estate of Nathan Oliveria

Frontispiece painting: *Portrait: Ambrose Bierce*
by J. H. E. Partington (1844–1899)

Bierce's Contemporary Shadow

ALTHOUGH HIS PRESUMED DEATH OCCURRED nearly a century ago, Ambrose Bierce casts a contemporary shadow. Literary critics have long compared the author of *The Devil's Dictionary* to classic satirists like Jonathan Swift. But in our time, Bierce, as a provocateur beholden to no one, bears a more striking resemblance to the revolutionary comic of the 1950s and '60s, Lenny Bruce.

More than a century ago, Bierce said that in this country satire "never had more than a sickly and uncertain existence, for the soul of it is wit, wherein we are dolefully deficient."

"Satire," said Lenny Bruce in the 1960s, "is tragedy plus time. You give it enough time, the public, the reviewers will allow you to satirize it." Is it still too soon for Americans to absorb the barbs of Bierce and Bruce without demonizing them as misanthropic or drug-addled?

Ambrose Bierce began knocking out satirical definitions for his San Francisco newspaper columns nearly a hundred years before Lenny Bruce was arrested in a North Beach nightclub for using honest Anglo-Saxon words like cocksucker and motherfucker, words that cry out for proper Biercean definitions.

While Bierce's bosses, including William Randolph Hearst, met his demand that not a single word that he wrote be altered, Bruce went to jail, demanding his right to use uncensored speech.

Although Bierce may not have admitted it, he would have enjoyed Bruce's stand-up bit, "Religion, Inc." Bierce defined religion as "a daughter of Hope and Fear, explaining to Ignorance the nature of the Unknowable." I can hear him chuckling out loud at Bruce's line: "If Jesus were killed twenty years ago, Catholic school children would wear little electric chairs around their necks, instead of crosses."

For both Bierce and Bruce, language became the prime tool with which to hammer away at the hypocrisy of humankind. Although they were each accused of being bitter, both men, in the guise of humor, engaged in serious work.

"All my humor," said Lenny Bruce, "is based upon destruction and despair. If the whole world were tranquil, without disease and violence, I'd be standing on the breadline right in back of J. Edgar Hoover."

Ambrose Bierce's world, like ours, is filled with treachery and despair, but his analysis of it, through elegant and brilliantly efficient definitions sheathed in language that is at once lucid and beguiling, remains a marvel.

Bierce defined corporation as "an ingenious device for obtaining individual profit without individual responsibility," a definition which has seasoned with time, not aged.

What may be most surprising about reading Bierce's dictionary now is how endlessly funny it is. Those capable of honesty will recognize themselves, just as Bierce saw himself, in these definitions. He defined egotist, which he was often accused of being, as "a person of low taste, more interested in himself than in me." The readers who will most enjoy Bierce's dictionary are those capable of recognizing that there is nobody funnier than the character in the mirror.

Compiling *The Best of the Devil's Dictionary* was a wholly pleasurable exercise in cherry-picking. I admit to looking over my shoulder occasionally for the ghost of old Bierce, with Civil War revolver, as I took a knife to much of the doggerel and extended commentary contributed by his invented poets and scholars, and pruned some of the lexicographer's more ponderous definitions. My crime is tempered by the fact that the full, unedited edition of *The Devil's Dictionary* is available at no cost online and through the usual e-book purveyors.

This streamlined edition includes extended definitions of such essential Bierce vocabulary as idiot, infidel, and regalia, definitions that deserve to be read out loud to fully appreciate their wisdom and lunacy, as well as the glory of their language. This volume offers readers a surprisingly contemporary hit parade of Bierce, suitable for easy reference and quotability.

To extend the spirit of Ambrose Bierce's lexicography as a living dictionary, we have compiled and included a list of 300+ words that we wish Bierce had defined. Some of these words did not exist in Bierce's time, others have taken on fresh meanings. Imagining Bierce's definitions is an amusing exercise and underscores how the essence of a culture resides in its language.

For a *Twenty-First Century Devil's Dictionary* that we hope to publish in 2012, we invite readers to contribute vital words and Biercean definitions at our website, www.kellyscovepress.com.

Bart Schneider
August, 2011

Abasement, *n.* A decent and customary mental attitude in the presence of wealth or power. Peculiarly appropriate in an employee when addressing an employer.

Abdication, *n.* An act whereby a sovereign attests his sense of the high temperature of the throne.

Abdomen, *n.* The temple of the god Stomach, in whose worship, with sacrificial rights, all true men engage.

Ability, *n.* The natural equipment to accomplish some small part of the meaner ambitions distinguishing able men from dead ones. In the last analysis ability is commonly found to consist mainly in a high degree of solemnity. Perhaps, however, this impressive quality is rightly appraised; it is no easy task to be solemn.

Abnormal, *adj.* Not conforming to standard. In matters of thought and conduct, to be independent is to be abnormal, to be abnormal is to be detested.

Aborigines, *n.* Persons of little worth found cumbering the soil of a newly discovered country. They soon cease to cumber; they fertilize.

Abrupt, *adj.* Sudden, without ceremony, like the arrival of a cannon-shot and the departure of the soldier whose interests are most affected by it. Dr. Samuel Johnson beautifully said of another author's ideas that they were "concatenated without abruption."

Abscond, *v.i.* To "move in a mysterious way," commonly with the property of another.

Abstainer, *n.* A weak person who yields to the temptation of denying himself a pleasure. A total abstainer is one who abstains from everything but abstention, and especially from inactivity in the affairs of others.

Absurdity, *n.* A statement or belief manifestly inconsistent with one's own opinion.

Academe, *n.* An ancient school where morality and philosophy were taught.

Academy, *n.* [from ACADEME] A modern school where football is taught.

Accomplice, *n.* One associated with another in a crime, having guilty knowledge and complicity, as an attorney who defends a criminal, knowing him guilty. This view of the attorney's position in the matter has not hitherto commanded the assent of attorneys, no one having offered them a fee for assenting.

Accordion, *n.* An instrument in harmony with the sentiments of an assassin.

Achievement, *n.* The death of endeavor and the birth of disgust.

Acquaintance, *n.* A person whom we know well enough to borrow from, but not well enough to lend to. A degree of friendship called slight when its object is poor or obscure, and intimate when he is rich or famous.

Adherent, *n.* A follower who has not yet obtained all that he expects to get.

Admiral, *n.* That part of a war-ship which does the talking while the figure-head does the thinking.

Admiration, *n.* Our polite recognition of another's resemblance to ourselves.

Admonition, *n.* Gentle reproof, as with a meat-axe. Friendly warning.

African, *n.* A nigger that votes our way.

Age, *n.* That period of life in which we compound for the vices that we still cherish by reviling those that we have no longer the enterprise to commit.

Air, *n.* A nutritious substance supplied by a bountiful Providence for the fattening of the poor.

Alderman, *n.* An ingenious criminal who covers his secret thieving with a pretence of open marauding.

Alliance, *n.* In international politics, the union of two thieves who have their hands so deeply inserted in each other's pockets that they cannot separately plunder a third.

Alone, *adj.* In bad company.

Ambidextrous, *adj.* Able to pick with equal skill a right-hand pocket or a left.

Ambition, *n.* An overmastering desire to be vilified by enemies while living and made ridiculous by friends when dead.

Amnesty, *n.* The state's magnanimity to those offenders whom it would be too expensive to punish.

Aphorism, *n.* Predigested wisdom.

Apologize, *v.i.* To lay the foundation for a future offence.

Apostate, *n.* A leech who, having penetrated the shell of a turtle only to find that the creature has long been dead, deems it expedient to form a new attachment to a fresh turtle.

Appeal, *v.t.* In law, to put the dice into the box for another throw.

Appetite, *n.* An instinct thoughtfully implanted by Providence as a solution to the labor question.

Applause, *n.* The echo of a platitude.

April Fool, *n.* The March fool with another month added to his folly.

Ardor, *n.* The quality that distinguishes love without knowledge.

Armor, *n.* The kind of clothing worn by a man whose tailor is a blacksmith.

Ass, *n.* A public singer with a good voice but no ear. In Virginia City, Nevada, he is called the Washoe Canary, in Dakota, the Senator, and everywhere the Donkey. The animal is widely and variously celebrated in the literature, art and religion of every age and country; no other so engages and fires the human imagination as this noble vertebrate.

Auctioneer, *n.* The man who proclaims with a hammer that he has picked a pocket with his tongue.

B

Babe or Baby, *n.* A misshapen creature of no particular age, sex, or condition, chiefly remarkable for the violence of the sympathies and antipathies it excites in others, itself without sentiment or emotion. There have been famous babes; for example, little Moses, from whose adventure in the bulrushes the Egyptian hierophants of seven centuries before doubtless derived their idle tale of the child Osiris being preserved on a floating lotus leaf.

Bait, *n.* A preparation that renders the hook more palatable. The best kind is beauty.

Bath, *n.* A kind of mystic ceremony substituted for religious worship, with what spiritual efficacy has not been determined.

Battle, *n.* A method of untying with the teeth of a political knot that would not yield to the tongue.

Befriend, *v.t.* To make an ingrate.

Beg, *v.* To ask for something with an earnestness proportioned to the belief that it will not be given.

Beggar, *n.* One who has relied on the assistance of his friends.

Belladonna, *n*. In Italian a beautiful lady; in English a deadly poison. A striking example of the essential identity of the two tongues.

Bigot, *n*. One who is obstinately and zealously attached to an opinion that you do not entertain.

Birth, *n*. The first and direst of all disasters. As to the nature of it there appears to be no uniformity. Castor and Pollux were born from the egg. Pallas came out of a skull. Galatea was once a block of stone. Peresilis, who wrote in the tenth century, avers that he grew up out of the ground where a priest had spilled holy water. It is known that Arimaxus was derived from a hole in the earth, made by a stroke of lightning. Leucomedon was the son of a cavern in Mount Aetna, and I have myself seen a man come out of a wine cellar.

Blank-verse, *n*. Unrhymed iambic pentameters—the most difficult kind of English verse to write acceptably; a kind, therefore, much affected by those who cannot acceptably write any kind.

Bore, *n*. A person who talks when you wish him to listen.

Brandy, *n*. A cordial composed of one part thunder-and-lightning, one part remorse, two parts bloody murder, one part death-hell-and-the- grave and four parts clarified Satan.

Bride, *n*. A woman with a fine prospect of happiness behind her.

Brute, *n*. See HUSBAND.

Cabbage, *n.* A familiar kitchen-garden vegetable about as large and wise as a man's head.

Calamity, *n.* A more than commonly plain and unmistakable reminder that the affairs of this life are not of our own ordering. Calamities are of two kinds: misfortune to ourselves, and good fortune to others.

Callous, *adj.* Gifted with great fortitude to bear the evils afflicting another.

Cannibal, *n.* A gastronome of the old school who preserves the simple tastes and adheres to the natural diet of the pre-pork period.

Capital, *n.* The seat of misgovernment. That which provides the fire, the pot, the dinner, the table and the knife and fork for the anarchist; the part of the repast that himself supplies is the disgrace before meat. *Capital Punishment*, a penalty regarding the justice and expediency of which many worthy persons—including all the assassins—entertain grave misgivings.

Carnivorous, *adj.* Addicted to the cruelty of devouring the timorous vegetarian, his heirs and assigns.

Cat, *n.* A soft, indestructible automaton provided by nature to be kicked when things go wrong in the domestic circle.

Cemetery, *n.* An isolated suburban spot where mourners match lies, poets write at a target and stone-cutters spell for a wager.

Centaur, *n.* One of a race of persons who lived before the division of labor had been carried to such a pitch of differentiation, and who followed the primitive economic maxim, "Every man his own horse."

Childhood, *n.* The period of human life intermediate between the idiocy of infancy and the folly of youth—two removes from the sin of manhood and three from the remorse of age.

Christian, *n.* One who believes that the New Testament is a divinely inspired book admirably suited to the spiritual needs of his neighbor. One who follows the teachings of Christ in so far as they are not inconsistent with a life of sin.

Circus, *n.* A place where horses, ponies and elephants are permitted to see men, women and children acting the fool.

Clairvoyant, *n.* A person, commonly a woman, who has the power of seeing that which is invisible to her patron, namely, that he is a blockhead.

Clarinet, *n.* An instrument of torture operated by a person with cotton in his ears. There are two instruments that are worse than a clarinet—two clarinets.

Clock, *n.* A machine of great moral value to man, allaying his concern for the future by reminding him what a lot of time remains to him.

Comfort, *n.* A state of mind produced by contemplation of a neighbor's uneasiness.

Commerce, *n.* A kind of transaction in which A plunders from B the goods of C, and for compensation B picks the pocket of D of money belonging to E.

Compromise, *n.* Such an adjustment of conflicting interests as gives each adversary the satisfaction of thinking he has got what he ought not to have, and is deprived of nothing except what was justly due.

Compulsion, *n.* The eloquence of power.

Congratulation, *n.* The civility of envy.

Congress, *n.* A body of men who meet to repeal laws.

Connoisseur, *n.* A specialist who knows everything about something and nothing about anything else.

Conservative, *n.* A statesman who is enamored of existing evils, as distinguished from the Liberal, who wishes to replace them with others.

Consolation, *n.* The knowledge that a better man is more unfortunate than yourself.

Contempt, *n.* The feeling of a prudent man for an enemy who is too formidable safely to be opposed.

Controversy, *n.* A battle in which spittle or ink replaces the injurious cannon-ball and the inconsiderate bayonet.

Convent, *n.* A place of retirement for woman who wish for leisure to meditate upon the vice of idleness.

Corporation, *n.* An ingenious device for obtaining individual profit without individual responsibility.

Coward, *n.* One who in a perilous emergency thinks with his legs.

Craft, *n.* A fool's substitute for brains.

Critic, *n.* A person who boasts himself hard to please because nobody tries to please him.

Cupid, *n.* The so-called god of love. This bastard creation of a barbarous fancy was no doubt inflicted upon mythology for the sins of its deities. Of all unbeautiful and inappropriate conceptions this is the most reasonless and offensive. The notion of symbolizing sexual love by a semisexless babe, and comparing the pains of passion to the wounds of an arrow— of introducing this pudgy homunculus into art grossly to materialize the subtle spirit and suggestion of the work—this is eminently worthy of the age that, giving it birth, laid it on the doorstep of prosperity.

Curiosity, *n.* An objectionable quality of the female mind. The desire to know whether or not a woman is cursed with curiosity is one of the most active and insatiable passions of the masculine soul.

Cynic, *n.* A blackguard whose faulty vision sees things as they are, not as they ought to be. Hence the custom among the Scythians of plucking out a cynic's eyes to improve his vision.

D

Dance, *v.i.* To leap about to the sound of tittering music, preferably with arms about your neighbor's wife or daughter.

**awn**, *n.* The time when men of reason go to bed. Certain old men prefer to rise at about that time, taking a cold bath and a long walk with an empty stomach, and otherwise mortifying the flesh. They then point with pride to these practices as the cause of their sturdy health and ripe years; the truth being that they are hearty and old, not because of their habits, but in spite of them. The reason we find only robust persons doing this thing is that it has killed all the others who have tried it.

Day, *n.* A period of twenty-four hours, mostly misspent. This period is divided into two parts, the day proper and the night, or day improper—the former devoted to sins of business, the latter consecrated to the other sort. These two kinds of social activity overlap.

Debauchee, *n.* One who has so earnestly pursued pleasure that he has had the misfortune to overtake it.

Debt, *n.* An ingenious substitute for the chain and whip of the slave-driver.

Decide, *v.i.* To succumb to the preponderance of one set of influences over another set.

Defenseless, *adj.* Unable to attack.

Degradation, *n.* One of the stages of moral and social progress from private station to political preferment.

Delegation, *n.* In American politics, an article of merchandise that comes in sets.

Deliberation, n. The act of examining one's bread to determine which side it is buttered on.

Deluge, *n.* A notable first experiment in baptism which washed away the sins (and sinners) of the world.

Dentist, *n.* A prestidigitator who, putting metal into your mouth, pulls coins out of your pocket.

Deputy, *n.* A male relative of an office-holder, or of his bondsman. The deputy is commonly a beautiful young man, with a red necktie and an intricate system of cobwebs extending from his nose to his desk. When accidentally struck by the janitor's broom, he gives off a cloud of dust.

Destiny, *n.* A tyrant's authority for crime and fool's excuse for failure.

Diaphragm, *n.* A muscular partition separating disorders of the chest from disorders of the bowels.

Diary, *n.* A daily record of that part of one's life, which he can relate to himself without blushing.

Dictionary, *n.* A malevolent literary device for cramping the growth of a language and making it hard and inelastic. This dictionary, however, is a most useful work.

Die, *n.* The singular of "dice." We seldom hear the word, because there is a prohibitory proverb, "Never say die." At long intervals, however, some one says, "The die is cast," which is not true, for it is cut. The word is found in an immortal couplet by the eminent poet and domestic economist, Senator Depew:

A cube of cheese no larger than a die
May bait the trap to catch a nibbling mie.

Digestion, *n.* The conversion of victuals into virtues.

Diplomacy, *n.* The patriotic art of lying for one's country.

Discussion, *n.* A method of confirming others in their errors.

Disobedience, *n.* The silver lining to the cloud of servitude.

Distance, *n.* The only thing that the rich are willing for the poor to call theirs, and keep.

Dog, *n.* A kind of additional or subsidiary Deity designed to catch the overflow and surplus of the world's worship. This Divine Being in some of his smaller and silkier incarnations takes, in the affection of Woman, the place to which there is no human male aspirant. The Dog is a survival—an anachronism. He toils not, neither does he spin, yet Solomon in all his glory never lay upon a door-mat all day long, sun-soaked and fly-fed and fat, while his master worked for the means wherewith to purchase the idle wag of the Solomonic tail, seasoned with a look of tolerant recognition.

Dragoon, *n.* A soldier who combines dash and steadiness in so equal measure that he makes his advances on foot and his retreats on horseback.

Druids, *n.* Priests and ministers of an ancient Celtic religion which did not disdain to employ the humble allurement of human sacrifice. Very little is now known about the Druids and their faith. Pliny says their religion, originating in Britain, spread eastward as far as Persia. Caesar says those who desired to study its mysteries went to Britain. Caesar himself went to Britain, but does not appear to have obtained any high preferment in the Druidical Church, although his talent for human sacrifice was considerable.

Druids performed their religious rites in groves, and knew nothing of church mortgages and the season-ticket system of pew rents. They were, in short, heathens and—as they were once complacently catalogued by a distinguished prelate of the Church of England—Dissenters.

Dullard, *n.* A member of the reigning dynasty in letters and life. The Dullards came in with Adam, and being both numerous and sturdy have overrun the habitable world. The secret of their power is their insensibility to blows; tickle them with a bludgeon and they laugh with a platitude.

Duty, *n.* That which sternly impels us in the direction of profit, along the line of desire.

Eat, *v.i.* To perform successively (and successfully) the functions of mastication, humectation, and deglutition.

"I was in the drawing-room, enjoying my dinner," said Brillat-Savarin, beginning an anecdote.

"What!" interrupted Rochebriant; "eating dinner in a drawing-room?"

"I must beg you to observe, monsieur," explained the great gastronome, "that I did not say I was eating my dinner, but enjoying it. I had dined an hour before."

Eavesdrop, *v.i.* Secretly to overhear a catalogue of the crimes and vices of another or yourself.

Eccentricity, *n.* A method of distinction so cheap that fools employ it to accentuate their incapacity.

Economy, *n.* Purchasing the barrel of whiskey that you do not need for the price of the cow that you cannot afford.

Edible, *adj.* Good to eat, and wholesome to digest, as a worm to a toad, a toad to a snake, a snake to a pig, a pig to a man, and a man to a worm.

Editor, *n.* A person who combines the judicial functions of Minos, Rhadamanthus and Aeacus, but is placable with an obolus; a severely virtuous censor, but so charitable withal that he tolerates the virtues of others and the vices of himself; who flings about him the splintering lightning and sturdy thunders of admonition till he resembles a bunch of firecrackers petulantly uttering his mind at the tail of a dog; then straightway murmurs a mild, melodious lay, soft as the cooing of a donkey intoning its prayer to the evening star. Master of mysteries and lord of law, high-pinnacled upon the throne of thought, his face suffused with the dim splendors of the Transfiguration, his legs intertwisted and his tongue a-cheek, the editor spills his will along the paper and cuts it off in lengths to suit. And at intervals from behind the veil of the temple is heard the voice of the foreman demanding three inches of wit and six lines of religious meditation, or bidding him turn off the wisdom and whack up some pathos.

Education, *n.* That which discloses to the wise and disguises from the foolish their lack of understanding.

Egotist, *n.* A person of low taste, more interested in himself than in me.

Ejection, *n.* An approved remedy for the disease of garrulity. It is also much used in cases of extreme poverty.

Electricity, *n.* The power that causes all natural phenomena not known to be caused by something else.

Eloquence, *n.* The art of orally persuading fools that white is the color that it appears to be. It includes the gift of making any color appear white.

Embalm, *v.i.* To cheat vegetation by locking up the gases upon which it feeds. By embalming their dead and thereby deranging the natural balance between animal and vegetable life, the Egyptians made their once fertile and populous country barren and incapable of supporting more than a meager crew. The modern metallic burial casket is a step in the same direction, and many a dead man who ought now to be ornamenting his neighbor's lawn as a tree, or enriching his table as a bunch of radishes, is doomed to a long inutility. We shall get him after awhile if we are spared, but in the meantime the violet and rose are languishing for a nibble at his *gluteus maximus*.

Emotion, *n.* A prostrating disease caused by a determination of the heart to the head. It is sometimes accompanied by a copious discharge of hydrated chloride of sodium from the eyes.

Enthusiasm, *n.* A distemper of youth, curable by small doses of repentance in connection with outward applications of experience. Byron, who recovered long enough to call it "entuzy-muzy," had a relapse, which carried him off—to Missolonghi.

Envy, *n.* Emulation adapted to the meanest capacity.

Erudition, *n.* Dust shaken out of a book into an empty skull.

Ethnology, *n.* The science that treats of the various tribes of Man, as robbers, thieves, swindlers, dunces, lunatics, idiots and ethnologists.

Exception, *n.* A thing which takes the liberty to differ from other things of its class, as an honest man, a truthful woman, etc.

Exhort, *v.t.* In religious affairs, to put the conscience of another upon the spit and roast it to a nut-brown discomfort.

Experience, *n.* The wisdom that enables us to recognize as an undesirable old acquaintance the folly that we have already embraced.

Extinction, *n.* The raw material out of which theology created the future state.

Faith, *n.* Belief without evidence in what is told by one who speaks without knowledge, of things without parallel.

Famous, *adj.* Conspicuously miserable.

Fashion, *n.* A despot whom the wise ridicule and obey.

Felon, *n.* A person of greater enterprise than discretion, who in embracing an opportunity has formed an unfortunate attachment.

Female, *n.* One of the opposing, or unfair, sex.

Fib, *n.* A lie that has not cut its teeth. An habitual liar's nearest approach to truth: the perigee of his eccentric orbit.

Fiddle, *n.* An instrument to tickle human ears by friction of a horse's tail on the entrails of a cat.

Fidelity, *n.* A virtue peculiar to those who are about to be betrayed.

Finance, *n.* The art or science of managing revenues and resources for the best advantage of the manager. The pronunciation of this word with the i long and the accent on the first syllable is one of America's most precious discoveries and possessions.

Flag, *n.* A colored rag borne above troops and hoisted on forts and ships. It appears to serve the same purpose as certain signs that one sees and vacant lots in London— "Rubbish may be shot here."

Fly-speck, *n.* The prototype of punctuation. It is observed by Garvinus that the systems of punctuation in use by the various literary nations depended originally upon the social habits and general diet of the flies infesting the several countries. These creatures, which have always been distinguished for a neighborly and companionable familiarity with authors, liberally or niggardly embellish the manuscripts in process of growth under the pen, according to their bodily habit, bringing out the sense of the work by a species of interpretation superior to, and independent of, the writer's powers.

Fool, *n.* A person who pervades the domain of intellectual speculation and diffuses himself through the channels of moral activity. He is omnific, omniform, omnipercipient, omniscience, omnipotent. He it was who invented letters, printing, the railroad, the steamboat, the telegraph, the platitude and the circle of the sciences. He created patriotism and taught the nations war—founded theology, philosophy, law, medicine and Chicago. He established monarchical and republican government. He is from everlasting to everlasting—such as creation's dawn beheld he fooleth now. In the morning of time he sang upon primitive hills, and in the noonday of existence headed the procession of being. His grandmotherly hand was warmly tucked-in the set sun of civilization, and in the twilight he prepares Man's evening meal of milk-and-morality and turns down the covers of the universal grave. And after the rest of us shall have retired for the night of eternal oblivion he will sit up to write a history of human civilization.

Forgetfulness, *n.* A gift of God bestowed upon doctors in compensation for their destitution of conscience.

Fork, *n.* An instrument used chiefly for the purpose of putting dead animals into the mouth. Formerly the knife was employed for this purpose, and by many worthy persons is still thought to have many advantages over the other tool, which, however, they do not altogether reject, but use to assist in charging the knife.

Freedom, *n.* Exemption from the stress of authority in a beggarly half dozen of restraint's infinite multitude of methods. A political condition that every nation supposes itself to enjoy in virtual monopoly. Liberty. The distinction between freedom and liberty is not accurately known; naturalists have never been able to find a living specimen of either.

Friendless, *adj.* Having no favors to bestow. Destitute of fortune. Addicted to utterance of truth and common sense.

Friendship, *n.* A ship big enough to carry two in fair weather, but only one in foul.

Frying-pan, *n.* One part of the penal apparatus employed in that punitive institution, a woman's kitchen. The frying-pan was invented by Calvin, and by him used in cooking span-long infants that had died without baptism; and observing one day the horrible torment of a tramp who had incautiously pulled a fried babe from the waste-dump and devoured it, it occurred to the great divine to rob death of its terrors by introducing the frying-pan into every household in Geneva. Thence it spread to all corners of the world, and has been of invaluable assistance in the propagation of his sombre faith.

Funeral, *n.* A pageant whereby we attest our respect for the dead by enriching the undertaker, and strengthen our grief by an expenditure that deepens our groans and doubles our tears.

Future, *n.* That period of time in which our affairs prosper, our friends are true and our happiness is assured.

G

Gallows, *n.* A stage for the performance of miracle plays, in which the leading actor is translated to heaven.

Garter, *n.* An elastic band intended to keep a woman from coming out of her stockings and desolating the country.

Genealogy, *n.* An account of one's descent from an ancestor who did not particularly care to trace his own.

Generous, *adj.* Originally this word meant noble by birth and was rightly applied to a great multitude of persons. It now means noble by nature and is taking a bit of a rest.

Geographer, *n.* A chap who can tell you offhand the difference between the outside of the world and the inside.

Geology, *n.* The science of the earth's crust—to which, doubtless, will be added that of its interior whenever a man shall come up garrulous out of a well.

, *n.* The outward and visible sign of an inward fear.

Gnu, *n.* An animal of South Africa, which in its domesticated state resembles a horse, a buffalo and a stag. In its wild condition it is something like a thunderbolt, an earthquake and a cyclone.

Good, *adj.* Sensible, madam, to the worth of this present writer. Alive, sir, to the advantages of letting him alone.

Goose, *n.* A bird that supplies quills for writing. These, by some occult process of nature, are penetrated and suffused with various degrees of the bird's intellectual energies and emotional character, so that when inked and drawn mechanically across paper by a person called an "author," there results a very fair and accurate transcript of the fowl's thought and feeling. The difference in geese, as discovered by this ingenious method, is considerable: many are found to have only trivial and insignificant powers, but some are seen to be very great geese indeed.

Grammar, *n.* A system of pitfalls thoughtfully prepared for the feet for the self-made man, along the path by which he advances to distinction.

Gravitation, *n.* The tendency of all bodies to approach one another with a strength proportion to the quantity of matter they contain—the quantity of matter they contain being as-certained by the strength of their tendency to approach one another. This is a lovely and edifying illustration of how science, having made A the proof of B, makes B the proof of A.

Guillotine, *n.* A machine which makes a Frenchman shrug his shoulders with good reason.

Gunpowder, *n.* An agency employed by civilized nations for the settlement of disputes which might become troublesome if left un-adjusted. By most writers the invention of gunpowder is ascribed to the Chinese, but not upon very convincing evidence. Milton says it was invented by the devil to dispel angels with, and this opinion seems to derive some support from the scarcity of angels.

Habit, *n.* A shackle for the free.

Hades, *n.* The lower world; the residence of departed spirits; the place where the dead live.

Among the ancients the idea of Hades was not synonymous with our Hell, many of the most respectable men of antiquity residing there in a very comfortable kind of way. Indeed, the Elysian Fields themselves were a part of Hades, though they have since been removed to Paris.

Hag, *n.* An elderly lady whom you do not happen to like; sometimes called, also, a hen, or cat. Old witches, sorceresses, etc., were called hags from the belief that their heads were surrounded by a kind of baleful lumination or nimbus—hag being the popular name of that peculiar electrical light sometimes observed in the hair. At one time hag was not a word of reproach: Drayton speaks of a "beautiful hag, all smiles," much as Shakespeare said, "sweet wench." It would not now be proper to call your sweetheart a hag—that compliment is reserved for the use of her grandchildren.

Hand, *n.* A singular instrument worn at the end of the human arm and commonly thrust into somebody's pocket.

Handkerchief, *n.* A small square of silk or linen, used in various ignoble offices about the face and especially serviceable at funerals to conceal the lack of tears. The handkerchief is of recent invention; our ancestors knew nothing of it and intrusted its duties to the sleeve.

Happiness, *n.* An agreeable sensation arising from contemplating the misery of another.

Harangue, *n.* A speech by an opponent, who is known as an harrangue-outang.

Hash, *x.* There is no definition for this word—nobody knows what hash is.

Hatred, *n.* A sentiment appropriate to the occasion of another's superiority.

Hearse, *n.* Death's baby-carriage.

Heart, *n.* An automatic, muscular blood-pump. Figuratively, this useful organ is said to be the seat of emotions and sentiments—a very pretty fancy which, however, is nothing but a survival of a once universal belief. It is now known that the sentiments and emotions reside in the stomach, being evolved from food by chemical action of the gastric fluid. The exact process by which a beefsteak becomes a feeling—tender or not, according to the age of the animal from which it was cut; the successive stages of elaboration through which a caviar sandwich is transmuted to a quaint fancy and reappears as a pungent epigram; the marvelous functional methods of converting a hard-boiled egg into religious contrition, or a cream-puff into a sigh of sensibility—these things have been patiently ascertained by M. Pasteur, and by him expounded with convincing lucidity. (See, also, my monograph, *The Essential Identity of the Spiritual Affections and Certain Intestinal Gases Freed in Digestion*, 4to, 687 pp.) In a scientific work entitled, I believe, *Delectatio Demonorum* (John Camden Hotton, London, 1873) this view of the sentiments receives a striking illustration; and for further light consult Professor Dam's famous treatise on *Love as a Product of Alimentary Maceration.*

Heathen, *n.* A benighted creature who has the folly to worship something that he can see and feel.

Heaven, *n.* A place where the wicked cease from troubling you with talk of their personal affairs, and the good listen with attention while you expound your own.

Hebrew, *n.* A male Jew, as distinguished from the Shebrew, an altogether superior creation.

Helpmate, *n.* A wife, or bitter half.

Hermit, *n.* A person whose vices and follies are not sociable.

Historian, *n.* A broad-gauge gossip.

History, *n.* An account mostly false, of events mostly unimportant, which are brought about by rulers mostly knaves, and soldiers mostly fools.

Hog, *n.* A bird remarkable for the catholicity of its appetite and serving to illustrate that of ours. Among the Mahometans and Jews, the hog is not in favor as an article of diet, but is respected for the delicacy and the melody of its voice. It is chiefly as a songster that the fowl is esteemed; the cage of him in full chorus has been known to draw tears from two persons at once. The scientific name of this dicky-bird is *Porcus Rockefelleri.* Mr. Rockefeller did not discover the hog, but it is considered his by right of resemblance.

Homicide, *n.* The slaying of one human being by another. There are four kinds of homicide: felonious, excusable, justifiable, and praiseworthy, but it makes no great difference to the person slain whether he fell by one kind or another—the classification is for advantage of the lawyers.

Honorable, *adj.* Afflicted with an impediment in one's reach. In legislative bodies it is customary to mention all members as honorable; as, "the honorable gentleman is a scurvy cur."

Hope, *n.* Desire and expectation rolled into one.

> *Delicious Hope! when naught to man it left—*
> *Of fortune destitute, of friends bereft;*
> *When even his dog deserts him, and his goat*
> *With tranquil disaffection chews his coat*
> *While yet it hangs upon his back; then thou,*
> *The star far-flaming on thine angel brow,*
> *Descendest, radiant, from the skies to hint*
> *The promise of a clerkship in the Mint.*
> > —Fogarty Weffing

Hospitality, *n.* The virtue which induces us to feed and lodge certain persons who are not in need of food and lodging.

House, *n.* A hollow edifice erected for the habitation of man, rat, mouse, beetle, cockroach, fly, mosquito, flea, bacillus and microbe. *House of Correction*, a place of reward for political and personal service, and for the detention of offenders and appropriations. *House of God*, a building with a steeple and a mortgage on it. *House-dog*, a pestilent beast kept on domestic premises to insult persons passing by and appal the hardy visitor. *House-maid*, a youngerly person of the opposing sex employed to be variously disagreeable and ingeniously unclean in the station in which it has pleased God to place her.

Hovel, *n.* The fruit of a flower called the Palace.

> *Twaddle had a hovel,*
>   *Twiddle had a palace;*
>   *Twaddle said: "I'll grovel*
>   *Or he'll think I bear him malice"—*
> *A sentiment as novel*
>   *As a castor on a chalice.*

Humanity, *n.* The human race, collectively, exclusive of the anthropoid poets.

Humorist, *n.* A plague that would have softened down the hoar austerity of Pharaoh's heart and persuaded him to dismiss Israel with his best wishes, cat-quick.

Hurry, *n.* The dispatch of bunglers.

Husband, *n.* One who, having dined, is charged with the care of the plate.

Hypocrite, *n.* One who, professing virtues that he does not respect, secures the advantage of seeming to be what he despises.

I

I is the first letter of the alphabet, the first word of the language, the first thought of the mind, the first object of affection. In grammar it is a pronoun of the first person and singular number. Its plural is said to be We, but how there can be more than one myself is doubtless clearer to the grammarians than it is to the author of this incomparable dictionary. Conception of two myselfs is difficult, but fine. The frank yet graceful use of "I" distinguishes a good writer from a bad; the latter carries it with the manner of a thief trying to cloak his loot.

Iconoclast, *n.* A breaker of idols, the worshipers whereof are imperfectly gratified by the performance, and most strenuously protest that he unbuildeth but doth not reedify, that he pulleth down but pileth not up. For the poor things would have other idols in place of those he thwacketh upon the mazzard and dispelleth. But the iconoclast saith: "Ye shall have none at all, for ye need them not; and if the rebuilder fooleth round hereabout, behold I will depress the head of him and sit thereon till he squawk it."

Idiot, *n.* A member of a large and powerful tribe whose influence in human affairs has always been dominant and controlling. The Idiot's activity is not confined to any special field of thought or action, but "pervades and regulates the whole." He has the last word in everything; his decision is unappealable. He sets the fashions and opinion of taste, dictates the limitations of speech and circumscribes conduct with a dead-line.

Idleness, *n.* A model farm where the devil experiments with seeds of new sins and promotes the growth of staple vices.

Ignoramus, *n.* A person unacquainted with certain kinds of knowledge familiar to yourself, and having certain other kinds that you know nothing about.

Illustrious, *adj.* Suitably placed for the shafts of malice, envy and detraction.

Imagination, *n.* A warehouse of facts, with poet and liar in joint ownership.

Immoral, *adj.* Inexpedient. Whatever in the long run and with regard to the greater number of instances men find to be generally inexpedient comes to be considered wrong, wicked, immoral. If man's notions of right and wrong have any other basis than this of expediency; if they originated, or could have originated, in any other way; if actions have in themselves a moral character apart from, and nowise dependent on, their consequences—then all philosophy is a lie and reason a disorder of the mind.

Impartial, *adj.* Unable to perceive any promise of personal advantage from espousing either side of a controversy or adopting either of two conflicting opinions.

Impenitence, *n.* A state of mind intermediate in point of time between sin and punishment.

Impiety, *n.* Your irreverence toward my deity.

Imposition, *n.* The act of blessing or consecrating by the laying on of hands—a ceremony common to many ecclesiastical systems, but performed with the frankest sincerity by the sect known as Thieves.

Imposter, *n.* A rival aspirant to public honors.

Impunity, *n.* Wealth.

Income, *n.* The natural and rational gauge and measure of respectability, the commonly accepted standards being artificial, arbitrary and fallacious.

Incompatibility, *n.* In matrimony a similarity of tastes, particularly the taste for domination. Incompatibility may, however, consist of a meek-eyed matron living just around the corner. It has even been known to wear a moustache.

Indifferent, *adj.* Imperfectly sensible to distinctions among things.

Indigestion, *n.* A disease which the patient and his friends frequently mistake for deep religious conviction and concern for the salvation of mankind. As the simple Red Man of the western wild put it, with, it must be confessed, a certain force: "Plenty well, no pray; big bellyache, heap God."

Indiscretion, *n.* The guilt of woman.

Inexpedient, *adj.* Not calculated to advance one's interests.

Infancy, *n.* The period of our lives when, according to Wordsworth, "Heaven lies about us." The world begins lying about us pretty soon afterward.

Infidel, *n.* In New York, one who does not believe in the Christian religion; in Constantinople, one who does. A kind of scoundrel imperfectly reverent of, and niggardly contributory to, divines, ecclesiastics, popes, parsons, canons, monks, mollahs, voodoos, presbyters, hierophants, prelates, obeah-men, abbes, nuns, missionaries, exhorters, deacons, friars, hadjis, high-priests, muezzins, brahmins, medicine-men, confessors, eminences, elders, primates, prebendaries, pilgrims, prophets, imaums, beneficiaries, clerks, vicars-choral, archbishops, bishops, abbots, priors, preachers, padres, abbotesses, caloyers, palmers, curates, patriarchs, bonezs, santons, beadsmen, canonesses, residentiaries, diocesans, deans, subdeans, rural deans, abdals, charm-sellers, archdeacons, hierarchs, class-leaders, incumbents, capitulars, sheiks, talapoins, postulants, scribes, gooroos, precentors, beadles, fakeers, sextons, reverences, revivalists, cenobites, perpetual curates, chaplains, mudjoes, readers, novices, vicars, pastors, rabbis, ulemas, lamas, sacristans, vergers, dervises, lectors, church wardens, cardinals, prioresses, suffragans, acolytes, rectors, cures, sophis, mutifs and pumpums.

Influence, *n.* In politics, a visionary *quo* given in exchange for a substantial *quid*.

Injury, *n.* An offense next in degree of enormity to a slight.

Injustice, *n.* A burden which of all those that we load upon others and carry ourselves is lightest in the hands and heaviest upon the back.

Ink, *n.* A villainous compound of tannogallate of iron, gum-arabic and water, chiefly used to facilitate the infection of idiocy and promote intellectual crime. The properties of ink are peculiar and contradictory: it may be used to make reputations and unmake them; to blacken them and to make them white; but it is most generally and acceptably employed as a mortar to bind together the stones of an edifice of fame, and as a whitewash to conceal afterward the rascal quality of the material. There are men called journalists who have established ink baths which some persons pay money to get into, others to get out of. Not infrequently it occurs that a person who has paid to get in pays twice as much to get out.

Insurance, *n.* An ingenious modern game of chance in which the player is permitted to enjoy the comfortable conviction that he is beating the man who keeps the table.

Intimacy, *n.* A relation into which fools are providentially drawn for their mutual destruction.

Introduction, *n.* A social ceremony invented by the devil for the gratification of his servants and the plaguing of his enemies. The introduction attains its most malevolent development in this century, being, indeed, closely related to our political system. Every American being the equal of every other American, it follows that everybody has the right to know everybody else, which implies the right to introduce without request or permission.

Inventor, *n.* A person who makes an ingenious arrangement of wheels, levers and springs, and believes it civilization.

J is a consonant in English, but some nations use it as a vowel—than which nothing could be more absurd. Its original form, which has been but slightly modified, was that of the tail of a subdued dog, and it was not a letter but a character, standing for a Latin verb, *jacere*, "to throw," because when a stone is thrown at a dog the dog's tail assumes that shape. This is the origin of the letter, as expounded by the renowned Dr. Jocolpus Bumer, of the University of Belgrade, who established his conclusions on the subject in a work of three quarto volumes and committed suicide on being reminded that the j in the Roman alphabet had originally no curl.

Jealous, *adj.* Unduly concerned about the preservation of that which can be lost only if not worth keeping.

Jester, *n.* An officer formerly attached to a king's household, whose business it was to amuse the court by ludicrous actions and utterances, the absurdity being attested by his motley costume. The king himself being attired with dignity, it took the world some centuries to discover that his own conduct and decrees were sufficiently ridiculous for the amusement not only of his court but of all mankind. The jester was commonly called a fool, but the poets and romancers have ever delighted to represent him as a singularly wise and witty person. In the circus of to-day the melancholy ghost of the court fool effects the dejection of humbler audiences with the same jests wherewith in life he gloomed the marble hall, panged the patrician sense of humor and tapped the tank of royal tears.

The widow-queen of Portugal
  Had an audacious jester
Who entered the confessional
  Disguised, and there confessed her.

Justice, *n.* A commodity which is a more or less adulterated condition the State sells to the citizen as a reward for his allegiance, taxes and personal service.

Kill, *v.t.* To create a vacancy without nominating a successor.

King, *n.* A male person commonly known in America as a "crowned head," although he never wears a crown and has usually no head to speak of.

Kiss, *n.* A word invented by the poets as a rhyme for "bliss." It is supposed to signify, in a general way, some kind of rite or ceremony appertaining to a good understanding; but the manner of its performance is unknown to this lexicographer.

Kleptomaniac, *n.* A rich thief.

Labor, *n.* One of the processes by which A acquires property for B.

Land, *n.* A part of the earth's surface, considered as property. The theory that land is property subject to private ownership and control is the foundation of modern society, and is eminently worthy of the superstructure. Carried to its logical conclusion, it means that some have the right to prevent others from living; for the right to own implies the right exclusively to occupy; and in fact laws of trespass are enacted wherever property in land is recognized. It follows that if the whole area of terra firma is owned by A, B and C, there will be no place for D, E, F and G to be born, or, born as trespassers, to exist.

Language, *n.* The music with which we charm the serpents guarding another's treasure.

Lap, *n.* One of the most important organs of the female system—an admirable provision of nature for the repose of infancy, but chiefly useful in rural festivities to support plates of cold chicken and heads of adult males. The male of our species has a rudimentary lap, imperfectly developed and in no way contributing to the animal's substantial welfare.

Laughter, *n.* An interior convulsion, producing a distortion of the features and accompanied by inarticulate noises. It is infectious and, though intermittent, incurable. Liability to attacks of laughter is one of the characteristics distinguishing man from the animals—these being not only inaccessible to the provocation of his example, but impregnable to the microbes having original jurisdiction in bestowal of the disease. Whether laughter could be imparted to animals by inoculation from the human patient is a question that has not been answered by experimentation.

Lawyer, *n.* One skilled in circumvention of the law.

Laziness, *n.* Unwarranted repose of manner in a person of low degree.

Learning, *n.* The kind of ignorance distinguishing the studious.

Legacy, *n.* A gift from one who is legging it out of this vale of tears.

Lexicographer, *n.* A pestilent fellow who, under the pretense of recording some particular stage in the development of a language, does what he can to arrest its growth, stiffen its flexibility and mechanize its methods. For your lexicographer, having written his dictionary, comes to be considered "as one having authority," whereas his function is only to make a record, not to give a law. The natural servility of the human understanding having invested him with judicial power, surrenders its right of reason and submits itself to a chronicle as if it were a statue. Let the dictionary (for example) mark a good word as "obsolete" or "obsolescent" and few men thereafter venture to use it, whatever their need of it and however desirable its restoration to favor—whereby the process of improverishment is accelerated and speech decays. On the contrary, recognizing the truth that language must grow by innovation if it grow at all, makes new words and uses the old in an unfamiliar sense, has no following and is tartly reminded that "it isn't in the dictionary"—although down to the time of the first lexicographer (Heaven forgive him!) no author ever had used a word that was in the dictionary. In the golden prime and high noon of English speech; when from the lips of the great Elizabethans fell words that made their own meaning and carried it in their very sound; when a Shakespeare and a Bacon were possible, and the language now rapidly perishing at one end and slowly renewed at the other was in vigorous growth and hardy preservation—sweeter than honey and stronger than a lion—the lexicographer was a person unknown, the dictionary a creation which his Creator had not created him to create.

Liar, *n.* A lawyer with a roving commission.

Liberty, *n.* One of Imagination's most precious possessions.

Lickspittle, *n.* A useful functionary, not infrequently found editing a newspaper. In his character of editor he is closely allied to the blackmailer by the tie of occasional identity; for in truth the lickspittle is only the blackmailer under another aspect, although the latter is frequently found as an independent species. Lickspittling is more detestable than blackmailing, precisely as the business of a confidence man is more detestable than that of a highway robber; and the parallel maintains itself throughout, for whereas few robbers will cheat, every sneak will plunder if he dare.

Life, *n.* A spiritual pickle preserving the body from decay. We live in daily apprehension of its loss; yet when lost it is not missed. The question, "Is life worth living?" has been much discussed; particularly by those who think it is not, many of whom have written at great length in support of their view and by careful observance of the laws of health enjoyed for long terms of years the honors of successful controversy.

Limb, *n.* The branch of a tree or the leg of an American woman.

Litigant, *n.* A person about to give up his skin for the hope of retaining his bones.

Litigation, *n.* A machine which you go into as a pig and come out of as a sausage.

Liver, *n.* A large red organ thoughtfully provided by nature to be bilious with. The sentiments and emotions which every literary anatomist now knows to haunt the heart were anciently believed to infest the liver; and even Gascoygne, speaking of the emotional side of human nature, calls it "our hepaticall parte." It was at one time considered the seat of life; hence its name—liver, the thing we live with. The liver is heaven's best gift to the goose; without it that bird would be unable to supply us with the Strasbourg *pate.*

Logic, *n.* The art of thinking and reasoning in strict accordance with the limitations and incapacities of the human misunderstanding. The basic of logic is the syllogism, consisting of a major and a minor premise and a conclusion—thus:

Major Premise: Sixty men can do a piece of work sixty times as quickly as one man.

Minor Premise: One man can dig a posthole in sixty seconds; therefore—

Conclusion: Sixty men can dig a posthole in one second.

This may be called the syllogism arithmetical, in which, by combining logic and mathematics, we obtain a double certainty and are twice blessed.

Longevity, *n*. Uncommon extension of the fear of death.

Looking-Glass, *n*. A vitreous plane upon which to display a fleeting show for man's disillusion given.

Loquacity, *n*. A disorder which renders the sufferer unable to curb his tongue when you wish to talk.

Loss, *n*. Privation of that which we had, or had not. Thus, in the latter sense, it is said of a defeated candidate that he "lost his election"; and of that eminent man, the poet Gilder, that he has "lost his mind." It is in the former and more legitimate sense, that the word is used in the famous epitaph:

> *Here Huntington's ashes long have lain*
> *Whose loss is our eternal gain,*
> *For while he exercised all his powers*
> *Whatever he gained, the loss was ours.*

Love, *n*. A temporary insanity curable by marriage or by removal of the patient from the influences under which he incurred the disorder.

Lunarian, *n*. An inhabitant of the moon, as distinguished from Lunatic, one whom the moon inhabits. The Lunarians have been described by Lucian, Locke and other observers, but without much agreement. For example, Bragellos avers their anatomical identity with Man, but Professor Newcomb says they are more like the hill tribes of Vermont.

Machination, *n*. The method employed by one's opponents in baffling one's open and honorable efforts to do the right thing.

So plain the advantages of machination
It constitutes a moral obligation,
And honest wolves who think upon't with loathing
Feel bound to don the sheep's deceptive clothing.
So prospers still the diplomatic art,
And Satan bows, with hand upon his heart.

—R. S. K.

Mad, *adj*. Affected with a high degree of intellectual independence; not conforming to standards of thought, speech and action derived by the conformants from study of themselves; at odds with the majority; in short, unusual. It is noteworthy that persons are pronounced mad by officials destitute of evidence that themselves are sane. For illustration, this present (and illustrious) lexicographer is no firmer in the faith of his own sanity than is any inmate of any madhouse in the land; yet for aught he knows to the contrary, instead of the lofty occupation that seems to him to be engaging his powers he may really be beating his hands against the window bars of an asylum and declaring himself Noah Webster, to the innocent delight of many thoughtless spectators.

Magdalene, *n.* An inhabitant of Magdala. Popularly, a woman found out. This definition of the word has the authority of ignorance, Mary of Magdala being another person than the penitent woman mentioned by St. Luke. It has also the official sanction of the governments of Great Britain and the United States. In England the word is pronounced Maudlin, whence maudlin, adjective, unpleasantly sentimental. With their Maudlin for Magdalene, and their Bedlam for Bethlehem, the English may justly boast themselves the greatest of revisers.

Magic, *n.* An art of converting superstition into coin. There are other arts serving the same high purpose, but the discreet lexicographer does not name them.

Magnet, *n.* Something acted upon by magnetism.

Magnetism, *n.* Something acting upon a magnet.
The two definitions immediately foregoing are condensed from the works of one thousand eminent scientists, who have illuminated the subject with a great white light, to the inexpressible advancement of human knowledge.

Magnificent, *adj.* Having a grandeur or splendor superior to that to which the spectator is accustomed, as the ears of an ass, to a rabbit, or the glory of a glowworm, to a maggot.

Maiden, *n.* A young person of the unfair sex addicted to clewless conduct and views that madden to crime. The genus has a wide geographical distribution, being found wherever sought and deplored wherever found. The maiden is not altogether unpleasing to the eye, nor (without her piano and her views) insupportable to the ear, though in respect to comeliness distinctly inferior to the rainbow, and, with regard to the part of her that is audible, bleating out of the field by the canary—which, also, is more portable.

Male, *n.* A member of the unconsidered, or negligible sex. The male of the human race is commonly known (to the female) as Mere Man. The genus has two varieties: good providers and bad providers.

Malefactor, *n.* The chief factor in the progress of the human race.

Mammalia, *n.pl.* A family of vertebrate animals whose females in a state of nature suckle their young, but when civilized and enlightened put them out to nurse, or use the bottle.

Man, *n.* An animal so lost in rapturous contemplation of what he thinks he is as to overlook what he indubitably ought to be. His chief occupation is extermination of other animals and his own species, which, however, multiplies with such insistent rapidity as to infest the whole habitable earth and Canada.

Marriage, *n.* The state or condition of a community consisting of a master, a mistress and two slaves, making in all, two.

Martyr, *n.* One who moves along the line of least reluctance to a desired death.

Mausoleum, *n.* The final and funniest folly of the rich.

Mayonnaise, *n.* One of the sauces which serve the French in place of a state religion.

Me, *pro.* The objectionable case of I. The personal pronoun in English has three cases, the dominative, the objectionable and the oppressive. Each is all three.

Meander, *n.* To proceed sinuously and aimlessly. The word is the ancient name of a river about one hundred and fifty miles south of Troy, which turned and twisted in the effort to get out of hearing when the Greeks and Trojans boasted of their prowess.

Medicine, *n*. A stone flung down the Bowery to kill a dog in Broadway.

Meekness, *n*. Uncommon patience in planning a revenge that is worth while.

Mercy, *n*. An attribute beloved of detected offenders.

Mesmerism, *n*. Hypnotism before it wore good clothes, kept a carriage and asked Incredulity to dinner.

Metropolis, *n*. A stronghold of provincialism.

Millennium, *n*. The period of a thousand years when the lid is to be screwed down, with all reformers on the under side.

Mind, *n*. A mysterious form of matter secreted by the brain. Its chief activity consists in the endeavor to ascertain its own nature, the futility of the attempt being due to the fact that it has nothing but itself to know itself with.

Mine, *adj*. Belonging to me if I can hold or seize it.

Minister, *n*. An agent of a higher power with a lower responsibility. In diplomacy an officer sent into a foreign country as the visible embodiment of his sovereign's hostility. His principal qualification is a degree of plausible inveracity next below that of an ambassador.

Minstrel, *adj*. Formerly a poet, singer or musician; now a nigger with a color less than skin deep and a humor more than flesh and blood can bear.

Miracle, *n*. An act or event out of the order of nature and unaccountable, as beating a normal hand of four kings and an ace with four aces and a king.

Misdemeanor, *n*. An infraction of the law having less dignity than a felony and constituting no claim to admittance into the best criminal society.

Misfortune, *n.* The kind of fortune that never misses.

Miss, *n.* The title with which we brand unmarried women to indicate that they are in the market. Miss, Missis (Mrs.) and Mister (Mr.) are the three most distinctly disagreeable words in the language, in sound and sense. Two are corruptions of Mistress, the other of Master. In the general abolition of social titles in our country they miraculously escaped to plague us. If we must have them let us be consistent and give one to the unmarried man. I venture to suggest Mush, abbreviated to Mh.

Money, *n.* A blessing that is of no advantage to us excepting when we part with it. An evidence of culture and a passport to polite society. Supportable property.

Monkey, *n.* An arboreal animal which makes itself at home in genealogical trees.

Monosyllabic, *adj.* Composed of words of one syllable, for literary babes who never tire of testifying their delight in the vapid compound by appropriate googoogling. The words are commonly Saxon—that is to say, words of a barbarous people destitute of ideas and incapable of any but the most elementary sentiments and emotions.

Moral, *adj.* Conforming to a local and mutable standard of right. Having the quality of general expediency.

Mouse, *n.* An animal which strews its path with fainting women.

Mouth, *n.* In man, the gateway to the soul; in woman, the outlet of the heart.

Mulatto, *n.* A child of two races, ashamed of both.

Mustang, *n.* An indocile horse of the western plains. In English society, the American wife of an English nobleman.

Nectar, *n.* A drink served at banquets of the Olympian deities. The secret of its preparation is lost, but the modern Kentuckians believe that they come pretty near to a knowledge of its chief ingredient.

Negro, *n.* The *piece de resistance* in the American political problem. Representing him by the letter n, the Republicans begin to build their equation thus: "Let n = the white man." This, however, appears to give an unsatisfactory solution.

Neighbor, *n.* One whom we are commanded to love as ourselves, and who does all he knows how to make us disobedient.

Nepotism, *n.* Appointing your grandmother to office for the good of the party.

Noise, *n.* A stench in the ear. Undomesticated music. The chief product and authenticating sign of civilization.

Nose, *n.* The extreme outpost of the face. From the circumstance that great conquerors have great noses, Getius, whose writings antedate the age of humor, calls the nose the organ of quell. It has been observed that one's nose is never so happy as when thrust into the affairs of others, from which some physiologists have drawn the inference that the nose is devoid of the sense of smell.

Novel, *n.* A short story padded. A species of composition bearing the same relation to literature that the panorama bears to art. As it is too long to be read at a sitting the impressions made by its successive parts are successively effaced, as in the panorama. Unity, totality of effect, is impossible; for besides the few pages last read all that is carried in mind is the mere plot of what has gone before. To the romance the novel is what photography is to painting. Its distinguishing principle, probability, corresponds to the literal actuality of the photograph and puts it distinctly into the category of reporting; whereas the free wing of the romancer enables him to mount to such altitudes of imagination as he may be fitted to attain; and the first three essentials of the literary art are imagination, imagination and imagination. The art of writing novels, such as it was, is long dead everywhere except in Russia, where it is new. Peace to its ashes— some of which have a large sale.

November, *n.* The eleventh twelfth of a weariness.

Oblivion, *n.* The state or condition in which the wicked cease from struggling and the dreary are at rest. Fame's eternal dumping ground. Cold storage for high hopes. A place where ambitious authors meet their works without pride and their betters without envy. A dormitory without an alarm clock.

Obsolete, *adj.* No longer used by the timid. Said chiefly of words. A word which some lexicographer has marked obsolete is ever thereafter an object of dread and loathing to the fool writer, but if it is a good word and has no exact modern equivalent equally good, it is good enough for the good writer. Indeed, a writer's attitude toward "obsolete" words is as true a measure of his literary ability as anything except the character of his work. A dictionary of obsolete and obsolescent words would not only be singularly rich in strong and sweet parts of speech; it would add large possessions to the vocabulary of every competent writer who might not happen to be a competent reader.

Occident, *n.* The part of the world lying west (or east) of the Orient. It is largely inhabited by Christians, a powerful subtribe of the Hypocrites, whose principal industries are murder and cheating, which they are pleased to call "war" and "commerce." These, also, are the principal industries of the Orient.

Ocean, *n.* A body of water occupying about two-thirds of a world made for man—who has no gills.

Omen, *n.* A sign that something will happen if nothing happens.

Once, *adv.* Enough.

Opera, *n.* A play representing life in another world, whose inhabitants have no speech but song, no motions but gestures and no postures but attitudes.

Opiate, *n.* An unlocked door in the prison of Identity. It leads into the jail yard.

Opportunity, *n.* A favorable occasion for grasping a disappointment.

Oppose, *v.* To assist with obstructions and objections.

Optimism, *n.* The doctrine, or belief, that everything is beautiful, including what is ugly, everything good, especially the bad, and everything right that is wrong. It is held with greatest tenacity by those most accustomed to the mischance of falling into adversity, and is most acceptably expounded with the grin that apes a smile. Being a blind faith, it is inaccessible to the light of disproof—an intellectual disorder, yielding to no treatment but death. It is hereditary, but fortunately not contagious.

Optimist, *n.* A proponent of the doctrine that black is white.

Orthodox, *n.* An ox wearing the popular religious joke.

Overwork, *n.* A dangerous disorder affecting high public functionaries who want to go fishing.

Owe, *v.* To have (and to hold) a debt. The word formerly signified not indebtedness, but possession; it meant "own," and in the minds of debtors there is still a good deal of confusion between assets and liabilities.

Pain, *n*. An uncomfortable frame of mind that may have a physical basis in something that is being done to the body, or may be purely mental, caused by the good fortune of another.

Palace, *n*. A fine and costly residence, particularly that of a great official. The residence of a high dignitary of the Christian Church is called a palace; that of the Founder of his religion was known as a field, or wayside. There is progress.

Pantaloons, *n*. A nether habiliment of the adult civilized male. The garment is tubular and unprovided with hinges at the points of flexion. Supposed to have been invented by a humorist. Called "trousers" by the enlightened and "pants" by the unworthy.

Pantomime, *n*. A play in which the story is told without violence to the language. The least disagreeable form of dramatic action.

Passport, *n*. A document treacherously inflicted upon a citizen going abroad, exposing him as an alien and pointing him out for special reprobation and outrage.

Past, *n*. That part of Eternity with some small fraction of which we have a slight and regrettable acquaintance. A moving line called the Present parts it from an imaginary period known as the Future. These two grand divisions of Eternity, of which the one is continually effacing the other, are entirely unlike. The one is dark with sorrow and disappointment, the other bright with prosperity and joy. The Past is the region of sobs, the Future is the realm of song. In the one crouches Memory, clad in sackcloth and ashes, mumbling penitential prayer; in the sunshine of the other Hope flies with a free wing, beckoning to temples of success and bowers of ease. Yet the Past is the Future of yesterday, the Future is the Past of to-morrow. They are one—the knowledge and the dream.

Patience, *n.* A minor form of despair, disguised as a virtue.

Patriotism, *n.* Combustible rubbish read to the torch of any one ambitious to illuminate his name.

In Dr. Johnson's famous dictionary patriotism is defined as the last resort of a scoundrel. With all due respect to an enlightened but inferior lexicographer I beg to submit that it is the first.

Peace, *n.* In international affairs, a period of cheating between two periods of fighting.

Pedigree, *n.* The known part of the route from an arboreal ancestor with a swim bladder to an urban descendant with a cigarette.

Perseverance, *n.* A lowly virtue whereby mediocrity achieves an inglorious success.

Pessimism, *n.* A philosophy forced upon the convictions of the observer by the disheartening prevalence of the optimist with his scarecrow hope and his unsightly smile.

Philanthropist, *n.* A rich (and usually bald) old gentleman who has trained himself to grin while his conscience is picking his pocket.

Philistine, *n.* One whose mind is the creature of its environment, following the fashion in thought, feeling and sentiment. He is sometimes learned, frequently prosperous, commonly clean and always solemn.

Philosophy, *n.* A route of many roads leading from nowhere to nothing.

Phoenix, *n.* The classical prototype of the modern "small hot bird."

Phonograph, *n.* An irritating toy that restores life to dead noises.

Photograph, *n.* A picture painted by the sun without instruction in art. It is a little better than the work of an Apache, but not quite so good as that of a Cheyenne.

Phrenology, *n.* The science of picking the pocket through the scalp. It consists in locating and exploiting the organ that one is a dupe with.

Physician, *n.* One upon whom we set our hopes when ill and our dogs when well.

Physiognomy, *n.* The art of determining the character of another by the resemblances and differences between his face and our own, which is the standard of excellence.

Piano, *n.* A parlor utensil for subduing the impenitent visitor. It is operated by pressing the keys of the machine and the spirits of the audience.

Picture, *n.* A representation in two dimensions of something wearisome in three.

Piety, *n.* Reverence for the Supreme Being, based upon His supposed resemblance to man.

Pig, *n.* An animal *(Porcus omnivorus)* closely allied to the human race by the splendor and vivacity of its appetite, which, however, is inferior in scope, for it sticks at pig.

Pilgrim, *n.* A traveler that is taken seriously. A Pilgrim Father was one who, leaving Europe in 1620 because not permitted to sing psalms through his nose, followed it to Massachusetts, where he could personate God according to the dictates of his conscience.

Plagiarize, *v.* To take the thought or style of another writer whom one has never, never read.

Plan, *v.t.* To bother about the best method of accomplishing an accidental result.

Platitude, *n.* The fundamental element and special glory of popular literature. A thought that snores in words that smoke. The wisdom of a million fools in the diction of a dullard. A fossil sentiment in artificial rock. A moral without the fable. All that is mortal of a departed truth. A demitasse of milk-and-mortality. The Pope's-nose of a featherless peacock. A jelly-fish withering on the shore of the sea of thought. The cackle surviving the egg. A desiccated epigram.

Platonic, *adj.* Pertaining to the philosophy of Socrates. Platonic Love is a fool's name for the affection between a disability and a frost.

Please, *v.* To lay the foundation for a superstructure of imposition.

Pleasure, *n.* The least hateful form of dejection.

Plow, *n.* An implement that cries aloud for hands accustomed to the pen.

Plunder, *v.* To take the property of another without observing the decent and customary reticences of theft. To effect a change of ownership with the candid concomitance of a brass band. To wrest the wealth of A from B and leave C lamenting a vanishing opportunity.

Pocket, *n.* The cradle of motive and the grave of conscience. In woman this organ is lacking; so she acts without motive, and her conscience, denied burial, remains ever alive, confessing the sins of others.

Police, *n.* An armed force for protection and participation.

Politeness, *n.* The most acceptable hypocrisy.

Politician, *n.* An eel in the fundamental mud upon which the superstructure of organized society is reared. When he wriggles he mistakes the agitation of his tail for the trembling of the edifice. As compared with the statesman, he suffers the disadvantage of being alive.

Politics, *n.* A strife of interests masquerading as a contest of principles. The conduct of public affairs for private advantage.

Positive, *adj.* Mistaken at the top of one's voice.

Posterity, *n.* An appellate court which reverses the judgment of a popular author's contemporaries, the appellant being his obscure competitor.

Pray, *v.* To ask that the laws of the universe be annulled in behalf of a single petitioner confessedly unworthy.

Predicament, *n.* The wage of consistency.

Predilection, *n.* The preparatory stage of disillusion.

Prehistoric, *adj.* Belonging to an early period and a museum. Antedating the art and practice of perpetuating falsehood.

Prejudice, *n.* A vagrant opinion without visible means of support.

Prescription, *n.* A physician's guess at what will best prolong the situation with least harm to the patient.

Present, *n.* That part of eternity dividing the domain of disappointment from the realm of hope.

Presentable, *adj.* Hideously appareled after the manner of the time and place.

Preside, *v.* To guide the action of a deliberative body to a desirable result. In Journalese, to perform upon a musical instrument; as, "He presided at the piccolo."

Price, *n.* Value, plus a reasonable sum for the wear and tear of conscience in demanding it.

Projectile, *n.* The final arbiter in international disputes. Formerly these disputes were settled by physical contact of the disputants, with such simple arguments as the rudimentary logic of the times could supply—the sword, the spear, and so forth. With the growth of prudence in military affairs the projectile came more and more into favor, and is now held in high esteem by the most courageous. Its capital defect is that it requires personal attendance at the point of propulsion.

Proof, *n.* Evidence having a shade more of plausibility than of unlikelihood. The testimony of two credible witnesses as opposed to that of only one.

Proof-reader, *n.* A malefactor who atones for making your writing nonsense by permitting the compositor to make it unintelligible.

Prophecy, *n.* The art and practice of selling one's credibility for future delivery.

Prude, *n.* A bawd hiding behind the back of her demeanor.

Publish, *n.* In literary affairs, to become the fundamental element in a cone of critics.

Push, *n.* One of the two things mainly conducive to success, especially in politics. The other is Pull.

Quill, *n.* An implement of torture yielded by a goose and commonly wielded by an ass. This use of the quill is now obsolete, but its modern equivalent, the steel pen, is wielded by the same everlasting Presence.

Quiver, *n.* A portable sheath in which the ancient statesman and the aboriginal lawyer carried their lighter arguments.

Quorum, *n.* A sufficient number of members of a deliberative body to have their own way and their own way of having it. In the United States Senate a quorum consists of the chairman of the Committee on Finance and a messenger from the White House; in the House of Representatives, of the Speaker and the devil.

Quotation, *n.* The act of repeating erroneously the words of another. The words erroneously repeated.

Radicalism, *n.* The conservatism of to-morrow injected into the affairs of to-day.

Ramshackle, *adj.* Pertaining to a certain order of architecture, otherwise known as the Normal American. Most of the public buildings of the United States are of the Ramshackle order, though some of our earlier architects preferred the Ironic.

Rank, *n.* Relative elevation in the scale of human worth.

Rapacity, *n.* Providence without industry. The thrift of power.

Rational, *adj.* Devoid of all delusions save those of observation, experience and reflection.

Reading, *n.* The general body of what one reads. In our country it consists, as a rule, of Indiana novels, short stories in "dialect" and humor in slang.

Realism, *n.* The art of depicting nature as it is seen by toads. The charm suffusing a landscape painted by a mole, or a story written by a measuring-worm.

Reason, *n.* Propensitate of prejudice.

Reason, *v.i.* To weight probabilities in the scales of desire.

Reasonable, *adj.* Accessible to the infection of our own opinions. Hospitable to persuasion, dissuasion and evasion.

Rebel, *n.* A proponent of a new misrule who has failed to establish it.

Recollect, *v.* To recall with additions something not previously known.

Reconciliation, *n.* A suspension of hostilities. An armed truce for the purpose of digging up the dead.

Reconsider, *v.* To seek a justification for a decision already made.

Red-skin, *n.* A North American Indian, whose skin is not red—at least not on the outside.

Referendum, *n.* A law for submission of proposed legislation to a popular vote to learn the nonsensus of public opinion.

Reflection, *n.* An action of the mind whereby we obtain a clearer view of our relation to the things of yesterday and are able to avoid the perils that we shall not again encounter.

Reform, *v.* A thing that mostly satisfies reformers opposed to reformation.

Regalia, *n.* Distinguishing insignia, jewels and costume of such ancient and honorable orders as Knights of Adam; Visionaries of Detectable Bosh; the Ancient Order of Modern Troglodytes; the League of Holy Humbug; the Golden Phalanx of Phalangers; the Genteel Society of Expurgated Hoodlums; the Mystic Alliances of Georgeous Regalians; Knights and Ladies of the Yellow Dog; the Oriental Order of Sons of the West;

the Blatherhood of Insufferable Stuff; Warriors of the Long Bow; Guardians of the Great Horn Spoon; the Band of Brutes; the Impenitent Order of Wife-Beaters; the Sublime Legion of Flamboyant Conspicuants; Worshipers at the Electroplated Shrine; Shining Inaccessibles; Fee-Faw-Fummers of the inimitable Grip; Jannissaries of the Broad-Blown Peacock; Plumed Increscencies of the Magic Temple; the Grand Cabal of Able-Bodied Sedentarians; Associated Deities of the Butter Trade; the Garden of Galoots; the Affectionate Fraternity of Men Similarly Warted; the Flashing Astonishers; Ladies of Horror; Cooperative Association for Breaking into the Spotlight; Dukes of Eden; Disciples Militant of the Hidden Faith; Knights-Champions of the Domestic Dog; the Holy Gregarians; the Resolute Optimists; the Ancient Sodality of Inhospitable Hogs; Associated Sovereigns of Mendacity; Dukes-Guardian of the Mystic Cess-Pool; the Society for Prevention of Prevalence; Kings of Drink; Polite Federation of Gents-Consequential; the Mysterious Order of the Undecipherable Scroll; Uniformed Rank of Lousy Cats; Monarchs of Worth and Hunger; Sons of the South Star; Prelates of the Tub-and-Sword.

Religion, *n.* A daughter of Hope and Fear, explaining to Ignorance the nature of the Unknowable.

Reliquary, *n.* A receptacle for such sacred objects as pieces of the true cross, short-ribs of the saints, the ears of Balaam's ass, the lung of the cock that called Peter to repentance and so forth. Reliquaries are commonly of metal, and provided with a lock to prevent the contents from coming out and performing miracles at unseasonable times. A feather from the wing of the Angel of the Annunciation once escaped during a sermon in Saint Peter's and so tickled the noses of the congregation that they woke and sneezed with great vehemence three times each.

Renown, *n.* A degree of distinction between notoriety and fame—a little more supportable than the one and a little more intolerable than the other. Sometimes it is conferred by an unfriendly and inconsiderate hand.

Reparation, *n.* Satisfaction that is made for a wrong and deducted from the satisfaction felt in committing it.

Repartee, *n.* Prudent insult in retort. Practiced by gentlemen with a constitutional aversion to violence, but a strong disposition to offend.

Repentance, *n.* The faithful attendant and follower of Punishment. It is usually manifest in a degree of reformation that is not inconsistent with continuity of sin.

Reporter, *n.* A writer who guesses his way to the truth and dispels it with a tempest of words.

Requiem, *n.* A mass for the dead which the minor poets assure us the winds sing o'er the graves of their favorites. Sometimes, by way of providing a varied entertainment, they sing a dirge.

Resident, *adj.* Unable to leave.

Resolute, *adj.* Obstinate in a course that we approve.

Respectability, *n.* The offspring of a *liaison* between a bald head and a bank account.

Resplendent, *adj.* Like a simple American citizen beduking himself in his lodge, or affirming his consequence in the Scheme of Things as an elemental unit of a parade.

Responsibility, *n.* A detachable burden easily shifted to the shoulders of God, Fate, Fortune, Luck or one's neighbor. In the days of astrology it was customary to unload it upon a star.

Retaliation, *n.* The natural rock upon which is reared the Temple of Law.

Retribution, *n.* A rain of fire-and-brimstone that falls alike upon the just and such of the unjust as have not procured shelter by evicting them.

Reveille, *n.* A signal to sleeping soldiers to dream of battlefields no more, but get up and have their blue noses counted. In the American army it is ingeniously called "rev-e-lee," and to that pronunciation our countrymen have pledged their lives, their misfortunes and their sacred dishonor.

Revelation, *n.* A famous book in which St. John the Divine concealed all that he knew. The revealing is done by the commentators, who know nothing.

Reverence, *n.* The spiritual attitude of a man to a god and a dog to a man.

Revolution, *n.* In politics, an abrupt change in the form of misgovernment. Specifically, in American history, the substitution of the rule of an Administration for that of a Ministry, whereby the welfare and happiness of the people were advanced a full half-inch. Revolutions are usually accompanied by a considerable effusion of blood, but are accounted worth it—this appraisement being made by beneficiaries whose blood had not the mischance to be shed. The French revolution is of incalculable value to the Socialist of to-day; when he pulls the string actuating its bones its gestures are inexpressibly terrifying to gory tyrants suspected of fomenting law and order.

Riot, *n.* A popular entertainment given to the military by innocent bystanders.

Rite, *n.* A religious or semi-religious ceremony fixed by law, precept or custom, with the essential oil of sincerity carefully squeezed out of it.

Road, *n.* A strip of land along which one may pass from where it is too tiresome to be to where it is futile to go.

Robber, *n.* A candid man of affairs.

Romance, *n.* Fiction that owes no allegiance to the God of Things as They Are. In the novel the writer's thought is tethered to probability, as a domestic horse to the hitching-post, but in romance it ranges at will over the entire region of the imagination—free, lawless, immune to bit and rein. Your novelist is a poor creature, as Carlyle might say—a mere reporter. He may invent his characters and plot, but he must not imagine anything taking place that might not occur, albeit his entire narrative is candidly a lie. Why he imposes this hard condition on himself, and "drags at each remove a lengthening chain" of his own forging he can explain in ten thick volumes without illuminating by so much as a candle's ray the black profound of his own ignorance of the matter. There are great novels, for great writers have "laid waste their powers" to write them, but it remains true that far and away the most fascinating fiction that we have is "The Thousand and One Nights."

Rostrum, *n.* In Latin, the beak of a bird or the prow of a ship. In America, a place from which a candidate for office energetically expounds the wisdom, virtue and power of the rabble.

Ruin, *v.* To destroy. Specifically, to destroy a maid's belief in the virtue of maids.

Rum, *n.* Generically, fiery liquors that produce madness in total abstainers.

Rumor, *n.* A favorite weapon of the assassins of character.

Saint, *n*. A dead sinner revised and edited.

Sandlotter, *n*. A vertebrate mammal holding the political views of Denis Kearney, a notorious demagogue of San Francisco, whose audiences gathered in the open spaces (sandlots) of the town. True to the traditions of his species, this leader of the proletariat was finally bought off by his law-and-order enemies, living prosperously silent and dying impenitently rich. But before his treason he imposed upon California a constitution that was a confection of sin in a diction of solecisms. The similarity between the words "sandlotter"and "sansculotte" is problematically significant, but indubitably suggestive.

Satan, *n*. One of the Creator's lamentable mistakes, repented in sashcloth and axes. Being instated as an archangel, Satan made himself multifariously objectionable and was finally expelled from Heaven. Halfway in his descent he paused, bent his head in thought a moment and at last went back.
　"There is one favor that I should like to ask," said he.
　"Name it."
　"Man, I understand, is about to be created. He will need laws."
　"What, wretch! you his appointed adversary, charged from the dawn of eternity with hatred of his soul—you ask for the right to make his laws?"
　"Pardon; what I have to ask is that he be permitted to make them himself."
　It was so ordered.

Satiety, *n.* The feeling that one has for the plate after he has eaten its contents, madam.

Satire, *n.* An obsolete kind of literary composition in which the vices and follies of the author's enemies were expounded with imperfect tenderness. In this country satire never had more than a sickly and uncertain existence, for the soul of it is wit, wherein we are dolefully deficient, the humor that we mistake for it, like all humor, being tolerant and sympathetic. Moreover, although Americans are "endowed by their Creator" with abundant vice and folly, it is not generally known that these are reprehensible qualities, wherefore the satirist is popularly regarded as a soul-spirited knave, and his every victim's outcry for codefendants evokes a national assent.

Sauce, *n.* The one infallible sign of civilization and enlightenment. A people with no sauces has one thousand vices; a people with one sauce has only nine hundred and ninety-nine. For every sauce invented and accepted a vice is renounced and forgiven.

Saw, *n.* A trite popular saying, or proverb. (Figurative and colloquial.) So called because it makes its way into a wooden head. Following are examples of old saws fitted with new teeth.

> *A penny saved is a penny to squander.*
> *A man is known by the company that he organizes.*
> *A bad workman quarrels with the man who calls him that.*
> *A bird in the hand is worth what it will bring.*
> *Better late than before anybody has invited you.*
> *Example is better than following it.*
> *Half a loaf is better than a whole one if there is much else.*
> *Think twice before you speak to a friend in need.*

What is worth doing is worth the trouble of asking some-
body to do it.
Least said is soonest disavowed.
He laughs best who laughs least.
Speak of the Devil and he will hear about it.
Of two evils choose to be the least.
Strike while your employer has a big contract.
Where there's a will there's a won't.

Scribbler, *n.* A professional writer whose views are antago-
nistic to one's own.

Scriptures, *n.* The sacred books of our holy religion, as distinguished from the false and profane writings on which all
other faiths are based.

Self-esteem, *n.* An erroneous
appraisement.

Self-evident, *adj.* Evident to one's self and to nobody else.

Selfish, *adj.* Devoid of consideration for the selfishness of others.

Siren, *n.* One of several musical prodigies famous for a vain
attempt to dissuade Odysseus from a life on the ocean wave.
Figuratively, any lady of splendid promise, dissembled purpose and disappointing performance.

Slang, *n.* The grunt of the human hog (*Pignoramus intolerabilis*)
with an audible memory. The speech of one who utters with
his tongue what he thinks with his ear, and feels the pride of a
creator in accomplishing the feat of a parrot. A means (under
Providence) of setting up as a wit without a capital of sense.

Sophistry, *n.* The controversial method of an opponent, distinguished from one's own by superior insincerity and fool-
ing. This method is that of the later Sophists, a Grecian sect

of philosophers who began by teaching wisdom, prudence, science, art and, in brief, whatever men ought to know, but lost themselves in a maze of quibbles and a fog of words.

Sorcery, *n.* The ancient prototype and forerunner of political influence. It was, however, deemed less respectable and sometimes was punished by torture and death.

Success, *n.* The one unpardonable sin against one's fellows.

Sycophant, *n.* One who approaches Greatness on his belly so that he may not be commanded to turn and be kicked. He is sometimes an editor.

Syllogism, *n.* A logical formula consisting of a major and a minor assumption and an inconsequent. (See LOGIC.)

Take, *v.t.* To acquire, frequently by force but preferably by stealth.

Talk, *v.t.* To commit an indiscretion without temptation, from an impulse without purpose.

Tariff, *n.* A scale of taxes on imports, designed to protect the domestic producer against the greed of his consumer.

Teetotaler, *n.* One who abstains from strong drink, sometimes totally, sometimes tolerably totally.

Telephone, *n.* An invention of the devil which abrogates some of the advantages of making a disagreeable person keep his distance.

Telescope, *n.* A device having a relation to the eye similar to that of the telephone to the ear, enabling distant objects to plague us with a multitude of needless details. Luckily it is unprovided with a bell summoning us to the sacrifice.

Tomb, *n.* The House of Indifference.

Tope, *v.* To tipple, booze, swill, soak, guzzle, lush, bib, or swig. In the individual, toping is regarded with disesteem, but toping nations are in the forefront of civilization and power.

Tree, *n.* A tall vegetable intended by nature to serve as a penal apparatus, though through a miscarriage of justice most trees bear only a negligible fruit, or none at all. When naturally fruited, the tree is a beneficent agency of civilization and an important factor in public morals. In the stern West and the sensitive South its fruit (white and black respectively) though not eaten, is agreeable to the public taste and, though not exported, profitable to the general welfare.

Trial, *n.* A formal inquiry designed to prove and put upon record the blameless characters of judges, advocates and jurors. In order to effect this purpose it is necessary to supply a contrast in the person of one who is called the defendant, the prisoner, or the accused. If the contrast is made sufficiently clear this person is made to undergo such an affliction as will give the virtuous gentlemen a comfortable sense of their immunity, added to that of their worth. In our day the accused is usually a human being, or a socialist, but in mediaeval times, animals, fishes, reptiles and insects were brought to trial.

Truce, *n.* Friendship.

Truth, *n.* An ingenious compound of desirability and appearance.

Truthful, *adj.* Dumb and illiterate.

Twice, *adv.* Once too often.

Type, *n.* Pestilent bits of metal suspected of destroying civilization and enlightenment, despite their obvious agency in this incomparable dictionary.

Tzetze (or Tsetse) Fly, *n.* An African insect (*Glossina morsitans*) whose bite is commonly regarded as nature's most efficacious remedy for insomnia, though some patients prefer that of the American novelist (*Mendax interminabilis*).

Un-American, *adj.* Wicked, intolerable, heathenish.

Understanding, *n.* A cerebral secretion that enables one having it to know a house from a horse by the roof on the house. Its nature and laws have been exhaustively expounded by Locke, who rode a house, and Kant, who lived in a horse.

Unitarian, *n.* One who denies the divinity of a Trinitarian.

Universalist, *n.* One who forgoes the advantage of a Hell for persons of another faith.

Valor, *n.* A soldierly compound of vanity, duty and the gambler's hope.

Vanity, *n.* The tribute of a fool to the worth of the nearest ass.

Virtues, *n.pl.* Certain abstentions.

Vituperation, *n.* Satire, as understood by dunces and all such as suffer from an impediment in their wit.

Vote, *n.* The instrument and symbol of a freeman's power to make a fool of himself and a wreck of his country.

 (double U) has, of all the letters in our alphabet,
the only cumbrous name, the names of the others being monosyllabic. This advantage of the
Roman alphabet over the Grecian is the more
valued after audibly spelling out some simple
Greek word, like *epixoriambikos*. Still, it is now
thought by the learned that other agencies than
the difference of the two alphabets may have
been concerned in the decline of "the glory that
was Greece" and the rise of "the grandeur that
was Rome." There can be no doubt, however,
that by simplifying the name of W (calling it
"wow," for example) our civilization could be, if
not promoted, at least better endured.

Wall Street, *n.* A symbol for sin for every devil to rebuke. That Wall Street is a den of thieves is a belief that serves every unsuccessful thief in place of a hope in Heaven.

War, *n.* A by-product of the arts of peace. The most menacing political condition is a period of international amity.

Weather, *n.* The climate of the hour. A permanent topic of conversation among persons whom it does not interest, but who have inherited the tendency to chatter about it from naked arboreal ancestors whom it keenly concerned.

Wedding, *n.* A ceremony at which two persons undertake to become one, one undertakes to become nothing, and nothing undertakes to become supportable.

White, *adj.* and *n.* Black.

Widow, *n.* A pathetic figure that the Christian world has agreed to take humorously, although Christ's tenderness towards widows was one of the most marked features of his character.

Wine, *n.* Fermented grape-juice known to the Women's Christian Union as "liquor," sometimes as "rum." Wine, madam, is God's next best gift to man.

Wit, *n.* The salt with which the American humorist spoils his intellectual cookery by leaving it out.

Witch, *n.* (1) Any ugly and repulsive old woman, in a wicked league with the devil. (2) A beautiful and attractive young woman, in wickedness a league beyond the devil.

Woman, *n.* An animal usually living in the vicinity of Man, and having a rudimentary susceptibility to domestication.

X in our alphabet being a needless letter has an added invincibility to the attacks of the spelling reformers, and like them, will doubtless last as long as the language. X is the sacred symbol of ten dollars, and in such words as Xmas, Xn, etc., stands for Christ, not, as is popular supposed, because it represents a cross, but because the corresponding letter in the Greek alphabet is the initial of his name—*Xristos.* If it represented a cross it would stand for St. Andrew, who "testified" upon one of that shape. In the algebra of psychology X stands for Woman's mind. Words beginning with X are Grecian and will not be defined in this standard English dictionary.

Yankee, *n.* In Europe, an American. In the Northern States of our Union, a New Englander. In the Southern States the word is unknown. (See DAMNYANK.)

Year, *n.* A period of three hundred and sixty-five disappointments.

Yesterday, *n.* The infancy of youth, the youth of manhood, the entire past of age.

Yoke, *n.* An implement, madam, to whose Latin name, *jugum*, we owe one of the most illuminating words in our language—a word that defines the matrimonial situation with precision, point and poignancy.

Youth, *n.* The Period of Possibility, when Archimedes finds a fulcrum, Cassandra has a following and seven cities compete for the honor of endowing a living Homer.

> *Youth is the true Saturnian Reign, the Golden Age on earth again, when figs are grown on thistles, and pigs betailed with whistles and, wearing silken bristles, live ever in clover, and cows fly over, delivering milk at every door, and Justice never is heard to snore, and every assassin is made a ghost and, howling, is cast into Baltimost!*
>
> —Polydore Smith

Z

Zany, *n.* A popular character in old Italian plays, who imitated with ludicrous incompetence the *buffone*, or clown, and was therefore the ape of an ape; for the clown himself imitated the serious characters of the play. The zany was progenitor to the specialist in humor, as we to-day have the unhappiness to know him. In the zany we see an example of creation; in the humorist, of transmission. Another excellent specimen of the modern zany is the curate, who apes the rector, who apes the bishop, who apes the archbishop, who apes the devil.

Zeal, *n.* A certain nervous disorder afflicting the young and inexperienced. A passion that goeth before a sprawl.

Zenith, *n.* The point in the heavens directly overhead to a man standing or a growing cabbage. A man in bed or a cabbage in the pot is not considered as having a zenith, though from this view of the matter there was once a considerably dissent among the learned, some holding that the posture of the body was immaterial. These were called Horizontalists, their opponents, Verticalists. The Horizontalist heresy was finally extinguished by Xanobus, the philosopher-king of Abara, a zealous Verticalist. Entering an assembly of philosophers who were debating the matter, hc cast a severed human head at the feet of his opponents and asked them to determine its zenith, explaining that its body was hanging by the heels outside. Observing that it was the head of their leader, the Horizontalists hastened to profess themselves converted to whatever opinion the Crown might be pleased to hold, and Horizontalism took its place among *fides defuncti.*

Twenty-First Century Devil's Dictionary

THE FOLLOWING LIST includes 300+ words that Ambrose Bierce did not define. Many of the words didn't exist in his time, while others have taken on fresh meanings as American culture has changed. We invite readers to visit the Bierce Cove at our website, www.kellyscovepress.com, to contribute Bierceian definitions to these words and add new words to the list. With the help of readers, Kelly's Cove Press hopes to publish the *Twenty-First Century Devil's Dictionary* in 2012.

Abortion
Adolescent
Aesthetics
Agitprop
Allegiance
Amnesty
Anachronism
Anarchist
Angst
Anorexic
Apathy
Armageddon
Art
Asshole
Attitude
Aura
Autism
Avatar

Awesome

Bailout
Baloney
Barbecue
Baseball
Bastard

Beatnik
Be-Bop
Beltway
Biblical
Bicoastal
Bionic
Bipolar
Bisexual

Bitch

Bling
Bliss
Blog
Blow-job
Blues
Blunt
Bonding
Branding
Brick-and-mortar
Bro
Browser
Brunch
Buff
Bullshit
Cancer

Caretaker
Carpool
Catharsis
Celebrity
Cellular
Charisma
Chauvinist
Chi
Chromosome
Cinema

Circumcision

Clone
Cock
Cocksucker
Codependent
Collateral Damage
Clitoris
Cloud
Comics
Committee
Compost
Comrade
Condom
Conservation
Constipation
Crack
Cross-dressing
Crush
Cubism
Cuckold
Cunt
Dealer
Decadent
Deficit
Delete
Depression
Diet
Digital

Dis
Disadvantaged
Disappear
Disassociation
Doppelgänger

Downward Dog

Dude
Dysfunction
E-book
Earth-mama
Ego
Embalm
Empathy
Empower
Enable
Erection
Espionage
Espresso
Exceptionalism
Exegesis
Exemption
Exfoliate
Existentialist
Expressionism
Expunge
Facelift
Faux
Feedback
Fixated
Flash Mob
Flyover
Fondle
Foodie

Footprint

Foreclosure
Freeway
Funk

Gaia

Gangsta

Gay

Genetic

Gentrify

Global Warming

Google

Gossip

Grapevine

Gratification

Gravity

Green

Grunge

Hemorrhoid

Herb

Heterosexual

Hip-Hop

Hipster

Holistic

Homie

Horny

Hybrid

Id

Illegal

Implant

Incest

Infertility

Insolent

Interface

Intervention

Invective

In Vitro Fertilization

Ironic

Jazz

Je ne sais quoi

Jive

Jock

Junk food

Karma

Laxative

Lesbian

Libertarian

Like

Literacy

Locavore

Mafiosa

Mammogram

Manic

Maoist

Master

Mastermind

Masturbate

Menopause

Mensch

Mentor

Meter Maid

Microwave

Middle Age

Mindshare

Modernism

Monogamy

Multicultural

Multiplex

Multitask

Muse

Nerd

Network

Neurotic

New Age

Nuke

Nymphomaniac

Obese

Oh My God

Okay

Online

Organic

Orgasm

Oxymoron
Partner
Pasta
Pedophile
Peripheral
Perspicacity
Pervert
Philanthropy
Piercing
Pimp
Pious
Polygamy
Postmodernism
Posttraumatic Stress
Preconception
Privacy
Proactive
Propaganda
Prosthetic
Psychedelic
Psychiatry
Punk
Pussy
Quark
Queen
Queer
Racism
Radical
Rap

Real-Time

Recession
Recycle
Reenactment
Regression
Relativity
Resonance
Ringtone
Risqué

Robot
Roommate
Sadomasochism
Salad bar
Salsa
Schadenfreude
Schizophrenia
Schmuck
Seminal
Sensual
Serendipity
Sexist
Sexuality

Sitcom

Skillset
Sleepover
Snitch
Sob Story
Social
Solar
Spam
Stalker
Steroids
Stress
String Theory
Stripper
Structuralism
Subprime
Suburbia
Subversion
Sugar Daddy
Superego
Surrogate
Sushi
Sustainability
Synergy
Systemic
Tactile

Tattoo
Taxes
Tea Party
Teen
Telecommunication
Terroir
Terrorism
Text
Thong
Toolkit
Totally
Tummy Tuck
Tweet
Twist-off
Ulcer
Unveil
Vacuum
Vagina
Vasectomy
Vegan
Verklempt
Video

Viral
Virus
Voyeur

Waterboard

Weird
Wellness
Widget
Wife Swapping
Wiki
Win-Win
Wired
Xenophobia
Yellowcake
Yin-Yang
Yoga
Yuppie
Zealot
Zeitgeist
Zen
Zionist
Zombie

Thanks to Anne, Catherine, Chester, Dorothea, Felix, Frances, Judith, Karl, Lorin, Pam, Sue, Steve, Teresa, and Theresa for helping to draft this list of words and reminding us that language and culture are inextricably connected.

Ambrose Bierce settled in San Francisco in 1867, at age twenty-five, two years after leaving the Army. He had fought in numerous Civil War skirmishes and was severely injured at Kennasaw Mountain. In San Francisco, Bierce found work at the mint and spent much of his spare time reading classic literature. By the next year he was writing for the *Golden Era* and the *News Letter*, of which he became editor. Bierce wrote for San Francisco-based publications for much of the next thirty years, with interludes in London and the Dakota Territory. He contributed thousands of columns, stories, sketches, criticism, and suites of definitions, which would become part of *The Devil's Dictionary*. In 1887, by then a celebrity journalist, he began working for William Randolph Hearst at the *San Francisco Examiner*.

Bierce was poorly published in book form. His volume of stories, *Tales of Soldiers and Civilians*, published in 1892, containing, arguably, the finest literary writing to grow out of the Civil War, had a limited distribution. In 1906, Doubleday, Page published the first collection of Bierce's definitions, titled *The Cynic's Word Book*. Bierce's Collected Works, in twelve volumes, began appearing in 1909. The editing as well as some of the writing was uneven, and the volumes were not widely available. In 1911, *The Devil's Dictionary* appeared as the seventh volume of Bierce's Collected Works.

Bierce disappeared in 1913, his last post sent the day after Christmas from Chihuahua, Mexico. Now, nearly a century later, as Ambrose Bierce celebrates his 169th birthday in an unknown location, The Library of America has published an 880-page volume of his work, and Kelly's Cove Press publishes *The Best of the Devil's Dictionary* and *Civil War Stories*.